ook at

anus

DATE DUE

GAYLORD   PRINTED IN U.S.A.

A Look at

Uranus

Salvatore Tocci

Franklin Watts

A DIVISION OF SCHOLASTIC INC.
NEW YORK · TORONTO · LONDON · AUCKLAND
SYDNEY · MEXICO CITY · NEW DELHI · HONG KONG
DANBURY, CONNECTICUT

TO MISTY,

*my steadfast companion who was with me throughout
the researching, writing, and revising of this book.*

Photographs © 2003: Corbis Images: 23, 27 (Bettmann), 32; FPG International/Getty Images/Michael Dunning: cover; NASA: 64 (H. Hammel/Massachusetts Institute of Technology), 41, 50, 52, 53, 56, 62, 72, 78, 81, 85 top right, 85 bottom, 86, 87, 88, 91, 103, 109 (JPL), 39, 94 (Erich Karkoschka/University of Arizona), 2, 17, 19, 44; North Wind Picture Archives: 20; Photo Researchers, NY: 10, 11 (David A. Hardy/SPL), 66, 104 (Pekka Parviainen/SPL), 25 (SPL); Photri Inc.: 15, 68, 74, 99 (NASA), 8, 29, 37, 48, 100.

Diagram p. 34 by Bernard Adnet

The photograph on the cover shows a false composite of Uranus. The photograph opposite the title page shows a montage of Uranus and its five major satellites.

Library of Congress Cataloging-in-Publication Data

Tocci, Salvatore.
  A look at Uranus / by Salvatore Tocci.
      p. cm. — (Out of this world)
Summary: Looks at the history and discovery of the planet Uranus.
Includes bibliographical references and index.
  ISBN 0-531-12250-6 (lib. bdg.)   0-531-15570-6 (pbk.)
  1. Uranus (Planet)—Juvenile literature. [1. Uranus (Planet)] I.
Title. II. Out of this world (Franklin Watts, Inc.)
  QB681.T63 2003
  523.47—dc21
                                        2002156020

1 2 3 4 5 6 7 8 9 10 R 12 11 10 09 08 07 06 05 04 03

Acknowledgments

I would like to thank Margaret W. Carruthers, planetary geologist, and Sam Storch, lecturer at the American Museum of Natural History's Hayden Planetarium, whose comments and suggestions were extremely helpful in revising my manuscript to that the content was not only accurate but current. My most sincere appreciation is reserved for Melissa Palestro, whose support and editorial insight have guided me through many projects on which we have worked together.

Contents

On September 20, 1977, *Voyager 2* was launched from the Kennedy Space Center at Cape Canaveral, Florida.

Chapter 1

Once-in-a-Lifetime Chance

On the morning of August 20, 1977, Earth and four other planets—Jupiter, Saturn, Uranus, and Neptune—were in just the right positions. Each of these planets travels around the Sun in a different orbit and at a different speed. But starting that August morning, each planet was exactly in the position in its orbit that the scientists at the National Aeronautics and Space Administration (NASA) had been waiting for. These five planets would continue to orbit this way for only a few weeks. The scientists also knew that this happened only once every 175 years. There was little time to lose.

At exactly 10:29 A.M. Eastern Daylight Time, a giant Titan III-E/Centaur rocket was launched from the Kennedy Space Center at

Cape Canaveral, Florida. Perched atop the rocket was an unmanned spacecraft called *Voyager 2*. *Voyager 1* would actually be launched from Cape Canaveral several weeks later. Although *Voyager 2* was launched first, it would be the second of the two spacecraft to reach Jupiter, their first destination in space.

Because Jupiter is about 500 million miles (800 million kilometers) from Earth, the trips for both *Voyager 1* and *Voyager 2* would be long ones. A car going 60 miles per hour (100 kph) would take 950 years to travel from Earth to Jupiter. Fortunately, the *Voyager* spacecraft traveled much faster than a car. Even though they were speeding to Jupiter at about 35,000 mph (56,000 kph), both spacecraft still took almost two years to reach the planet. *Voyager 1* finally arrived at Jupiter on March 5, 1979. *Voyager 2* arrived on July 9, 1979. Soon after their arrival, both spacecraft started sending close-up images of Jupiter back to Earth.

When they were finished looking at Jupiter, both spacecraft were then

Artist's impression of the *Voyager 1* spacecraft leaving Saturn after its encounter in November 1980

sent on to their next destination—Saturn. Once again, *Voyager 1* was the first to arrive. And once again, both spacecraft sent close-up images of Saturn back to Earth. When they were finished looking at Saturn, *Voyager 1* and *Voyager 2* went their separate ways. *Voyager 1* headed into

deep space with no more planets to visit. *Voyager 2*, however, had two more visits to make. After flying by Saturn, *Voyager 2* would be the first spacecraft to visit the seventh planet in orbit from the Sun—Uranus.

Shortening the Trip

Getting a spacecraft to fly by any planet closely enough to photograph it is no easy task. Getting one to Uranus was even more of a challenge. Uranus is about four times farther from Earth than Jupiter and twice as far as Saturn. If *Voyager 2* had been programmed to fly directly to Uranus from Earth, the journey would have taken thirty years. Instead, *Voyager 2* took only a little over eight years to get there. Both Jupiter and Saturn helped shorten the spacecraft's journey to Uranus.

As *Voyager 2* approached Jupiter, the spacecraft got some help from the planet's motion and its *gravity*. Gravity is a force that causes two objects to attract each other. When *Voyager 2* got close enough to Jupiter, the planet's gravity pulled the spacecraft into its orbit. While the space-craft was in orbit around Jupiter, it was also in the planet's orbit around the Sun. The speed at which *Voyager 2* was orbiting the Sun at this point was greater than the speed it had reached when it approached the planet. A signal was then sent to *Voyager 2* to boost the spacecraft out of Jupiter's orbit and send it on its way. Leaving Jupiter, *Voyager 2* was now travel-ing faster than when it had arrived at the planet.

The scientists knew that they had only a few weeks to launch the spacecraft from Earth. By the time *Voyager 2* reached Jupiter, the planet would be in perfect position in its orbit to help propel the spacecraft toward Saturn. In turn, Saturn would be in perfect position in its orbit when *Voyager 2* arrived to help speed the spacecraft on its journey to Uranus.

RTGs

Providing power to run all the equipment onboard a spacecraft has always been a challenge. The challenge becomes even greater when a spacecraft, like Voyager 2, must travel deep into space. Any spacecraft that journeys into deep space is too far from the Sun to depend on solar power to run its instruments.

To solve this problem, NASA developed Radioisotope Thermoelectric Generators (RTGs), which use radioactive elements such as plutonium. These radioactive elements spontaneously decay, or break apart, releasing heat. RTGs convert this heat into electricity, which powers the instruments aboard a spacecraft.

The RTGs onboard Voyager 2 contain about 40 pounds (18 kilograms) of plutonium. This plutonium is not a weapons-grade material that can be used to make nuclear bombs. In addition, the radiation given off by this plutonium cannot penetrate a piece of paper or your skin. Even so, the plutonium is shielded by layers of special materials to prevent any radioactive leakage, should there be an accident during the spacecraft's launch.

The electricity generated by the decay of the plutonium aboard Voyager 2 powers the spacecraft's computers, cameras, radios, sensors, and recording equipment. However, as the plutonium continues to decay, the power output of the RTGs is slowly decreasing. By 2010, there will be too little power to run all the instruments. NASA scientists will then use a power-sharing plan, turning on some instruments while turning off others. The scientists will continue to operate Voyager 2 this way for about another ten years. At that point, the RTGs will probably not produce enough power to run any of the instruments. By 2020, NASA will likely lose all contact with Voyager 2.

However, even with Jupiter's and Saturn's help, getting to Uranus still posed many problems. As Voyager 2 approached Uranus, the planet was 1.8 billion miles (2.9 billion km) from Earth. NASA scientists picked a target just inside the orbit of one of the moons circling Uranus. If all went according to plan, Voyager 2 would come within 60 miles (100 km) of this target. Having Voyager 2 hit its target was like trying to sink a golf ball in a hole that is 1,500 miles (2,400 km) away! Unlike a golf ball, Voyager 2 could still be controlled after it was launched. But hitting its target was still a tremendous challenge.

The great distance to Uranus posed another problem. NASA scientists used radio signals to control *Voyager 2*. By the time the spacecraft got to Uranus, each message they sent from Earth took two hours and forty-five minutes to reach the spacecraft. Any message that *Voyager 2* sent back took another two hours and forty-five minutes. As a result, the scientists did not know if their instruction had been carried out until five and a half hours after they first sent it. If *Voyager 2* failed to respond to an instruction, it might be too late to send another one.

Another problem *Voyager 2* had to overcome was the dim sunlight. In the vicinity of Uranus, the sunlight is nearly four hundred times dimmer than it is on Earth during daylight. The Sun is, on average, 93 million miles (150 million km) from Earth. From Earth, the Sun appears as a very large ball of bright light. However, the Sun is about 2 billion miles (3.2 billion km) from Uranus. From Uranus, the Sun appears as a small, brilliant star. The camera aboard *Voyager 2* could take a sharp picture of a newspaper headline from a distance of 1 mile (1.6 km). However, without enough light, the camera would not be able to "see" anything.

One way for a camera to get more light is to lengthen the time that its lens remains open. But *Voyager 2* was traveling at about 45,000 mph (70,000 kph) when it approached Uranus. If the lens were kept opened for just ten seconds, *Voyager 2* would have traveled 125 miles (200 km) in that short time. Any photographs that the spacecraft took would be blurred, just as they would be if you tried to take pictures from a moving car. To overcome this problem, the scientists programmed *Voyager 2* so that the whole spacecraft rotated slowly backward just enough to offset its forward motion. This is like panning a camera to keep up with a moving object so that you can get a clear picture.

The *Voyager* camera system

Picking Up the Signals

Even if the camera took clear pictures, there was another problem that the NASA scientists had to solve. The video images were first changed to radio signals before being sent back to Earth, where they were picked up by large antenna dishes. Because of the great distance that they traveled, these radio signals were very weak by the time they arrived on Earth. To appreciate how weak these signals were, consider that a digital watch today operates at an energy level one hundred billion times greater that the energy level of a radio signal coming from Uranus. Even the largest antenna dish in the world would not be able to pick up such a faint signal.

The only way to detect the radio signals from Uranus was to link a number of antenna dishes in California, Spain, and Australia to form one large system. Australia was the best place to receive the radio signals because of Uranus's position in the sky. At that time, the planet was in the region of the constellation Scorpius, which was best seen from the Southern Hemisphere. Therefore, the dishes in Australia could be aimed directly at *Voyager 2* as it passed by Uranus.

NASA scientists had been well aware of all the obstacles they had to overcome in order to get the first close-up look at Uranus. Plans to explore the outer *solar system,* which includes Jupiter, Saturn, Uranus, and Neptune, had begun in 1971. But in 1972, NASA had only enough money to send unmanned spacecraft to visit the two planets closest to Earth—Jupiter and Saturn. These spacecraft included *Pioneers 10* and *11* and *Voyagers 1* and *2.* In 1975, however, plans changed when NASA realized that in two years, all the planets of the outer solar system would be in just the right positions to have a spacecraft visit Uranus and Neptune. *Voyager 2* was selected to make that visit.

Each *Voyager* spacecraft was built from about sixty-five thousand individual parts. In turn, many of these parts were built from the same number of smaller parts such as transistors. As a result, the number of electronic circuits in each *Voyager* spacecraft equaled the number in some two thousand color televisions. Amazingly, all this electronic equipment operated on only four hundred watts of power, which is about one-tenth the power an average home uses to run all its electrical devices.

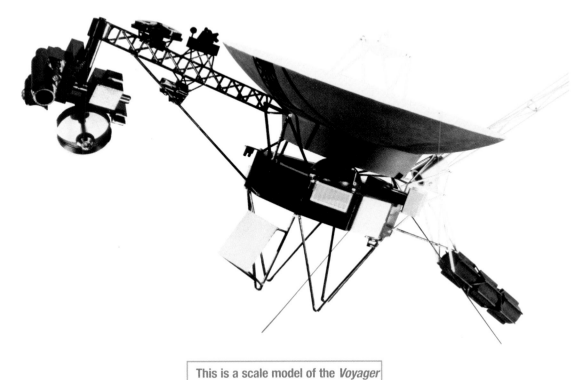

This is a scale model of the *Voyager* spacecraft.

One of the thousands of parts each *Voyager* contained was a tape recorder used to store the scientific information it collected and sent back to Earth. Because it had to record so much information, the tape had to be constantly rewound and then reused. The distance the tape moved back and forth as it recorded over and over again was about equal to the distance across the United States. This is like playing and then rewinding a two-hour cassette on your VCR once a day for the next twenty-two years without any problem.

Developing Problems

Soon after *Voyager 2* was launched, the system that received command signals from Earth failed. NASA scientists had to depend upon a backup system. But after *Voyager 2* left Saturn and headed for Uranus, this backup system also developed problems. In addition, the mechanism to adjust the spacecraft so that its camera could take clear pictures of Uranus was not working. Fortunately, the scientists had plenty of time to solve these problems. It would be nearly four and a half years before *Voyager 2* reached its next destination.

In November 1985, *Voyager 2* started its approach to Uranus. This marked the beginning of its Observatory Phase. Even though it was still about 65 million miles (105 million km) from Uranus, *Voyager 2* started sending back images. They were far better than anything that had been taken through a telescope on Earth. Uranus appeared as a greenish blue disc. However, no details such as the clouds or colored bands that *Voyager 2* had spotted on Jupiter and Saturn could be seen on Uranus.

In mid-January 1986, *Voyager 2* entered its Far Encounter Phase. At this point, the spacecraft was about 2 million miles (3.2 million km) from the planet. From this distance, its camera could get a better view of the planet's surface. During this phase, NASA scientists made final adjustments so that *Voyager 2* would hit its target when it arrived at Uranus. On January 22, 1986—some eight and a half years after it left Earth—*Voyager 2* entered its Near Encounter Phase. This phase lasted for only four days. During this time, the spacecraft flew within 68,000 miles (110,000 km) of Uranus and provided NASA with a lot of new information about the planet. Then, on January 26, 1986, *Voyager 2* entered its Post-Encounter Phase. Although it was still provid-

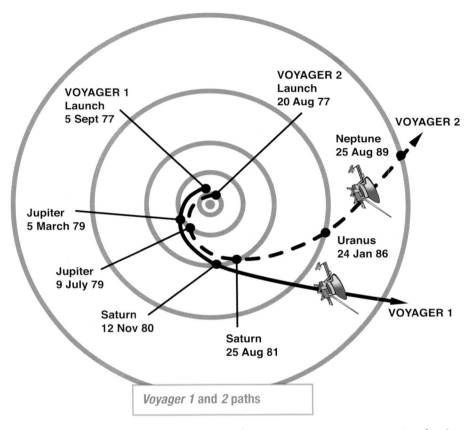

VOYAGER 1
Launch
5 Sept 77

VOYAGER 2
Launch
20 Aug 77

VOYAGER 2

Neptune
25 Aug 89

Jupiter
5 March 79

Uranus
24 Jan 86

Jupiter
9 July 79

Saturn
12 Nov 80

VOYAGER 1

Saturn
25 Aug 81

Voyager 1 and *2* paths

ing images of Uranus, the spacecraft was now on its way to its final destination—Neptune.

After traveling in space for some eight and a half years, *Voyager 2* spent only four months—November 1985 through February 1986— studying Uranus. During those four months, *Voyager 2* spent only four days—January 22 to January 26—getting a close look at the planet. During those four days, its closest look lasted for only a six-hour period on January 24. But from the start, and especially during those six hours, *Voyager 2* revealed many fascinating and unexpected secrets that Uranus had kept since it was first discovered.

William Herschel looks through the telescope that he and his sister, Caroline, built.

Chapter 2

Herschel's Discovery

Nearly two hundred years before *Voyager 2* started its trip to Uranus, William Herschel was looking through his telescope at the night sky. That night—March 13, 1781—Herschel was carefully measuring the positions of stars. Suddenly, he spotted one that appeared noticeably larger than the others. In addition, it did not shine like a star, as a point of light, but rather as a small disc. Herschel thought that he had discovered a *comet*. A comet is a small ball of rock and ice that travels in a long orbit around the Sun from the far edge of the solar system. Herschel reported his discovery to his fellow *astronomers*, or scientists who study outer space.

Night after night, Herschel kept studying this small disc of light as it moved through the sky. What he saw made him change his mind. It wasn't a comet after all. For one thing, it did not look hazy like a comet. Rather, its image was marked by a distinct border. The object also moved so slowly that Herschel concluded that it must be traveling well beyond the orbit of Saturn, which at that time was believed to be the outer boundary of our solar system. Because of their small size, no comets had ever been seen beyond Saturn's orbit. The object also traveled in an orbit that had a different shape from what comets normally follow. Herschel soon realized that the object he had spotted was not a comet. But for months, he had no idea what it was.

Then in July 1871, two other astronomers realized that Herschel had discovered a planet. This was a monumental discovery in astronomy. For almost two thousand years, people believed that all the planets that existed had been discovered. The ancient Greeks believed that there were seven planets in our solar system. These were the objects that moved or wandered through the sky, unlike the stars, which appear almost motionless. Because of their movement, these seven bodies in space were called planets, from the Greek word meaning "wanderer." The seven planets the Greeks counted included the Sun, the Moon, Mercury, Venus, Mars, Jupiter, and Saturn. All seven, they believed, revolved around the Earth, which was thought to be the center of the universe.

In 1543, that concept of the universe dramatically changed. That year, Nicolaus Copernicus, a Polish astronomer, published a book in which he said that the Sun, and not the Earth, was the center of our solar system. In Copernicus's model of our solar system, Mercury, Venus, Earth, Mars, Jupiter, and Saturn orbited the Sun. Only the Moon revolved around Earth. According to Copernicus, there were only six planets. This is the way most astronomers viewed our solar sys-

The Polish astronomer Nicolaus Copernicus is generally credited with proposing that Earth and the other planets were part of a solar system, in which they revolved around the Sun.

tem for the next 238 years. With Herschel's discovery of Uranus in 1781, he added to our solar system the first planet to be discovered in recorded history.

Naming the Planet

As its discoverer, Herschel was given the honor of giving this new planet a name. He proposed naming it after King George III of England, Herschel's adopted homeland. Throughout his life, Herschel referred to the new planet as Georgium Sidus, which is Latin for "George's Star." This name, however, was not accepted by other astronomers, especially those outside England. They pointed out that tradition called for naming planets after figures in Roman and Greek mythology.

Several astronomers proposed a name that made sense. Jupiter, the fifth planet from the Sun, was named after the king of the Roman gods. Saturn, the sixth planet, was named after Jupiter's father. Why not name the seventh planet after Saturn's father, who was the god of the heavens? In Greek myths, Saturn's father was Ouranos. The Latin spelling for this Greek god is "Uranus." The seventh planet from our Sun soon became known by everyone as Uranus.

Soon after Herschel discovered Uranus, many astronomers wondered why the planet had not been spotted earlier. Although it is some 1.7 billion miles (2.7 billion km) from Earth, Uranus can easily be spotted with a simple telescope. In fact, on a clear night, Uranus can even be seen with just one's eyes. True, you must have excellent eyesight, know exactly where to look in the night sky, and stare very hard to find it, but you can still pick it out from among the hundreds of stars that you would also see. Spotting Uranus with a telescope, especially a large one, should be easy. Then why didn't someone notice it sooner?

Actually, an astronomer had spotted Uranus almost one hundred years before Herschel did. On the night of December 23, 1690, an English astronomer named John Flamsteed observed what he thought was a star and recorded its position in his catalog. He gave it the name 34 Tauri because at that time it appeared to be in the constellation of Taurus the Bull. Calculations later showed that the position Flamsteed recorded was exactly the position of Uranus that night. Entries in his catalog revealed that he later spotted Uranus five more times—once in 1713 and four times in 1715. The record for spotting Uranus, however, goes to a

Although he is believed to be the first person to sight Uranus, the English astronomer John Flamsteed had very little scientific training.

French astronomer named Pierre Charles Le Monnier. Between 1764 and 1771, he recorded seeing Uranus on thirteen different nights. Like Flamsteed, he thought that what he was looking at was a star.

Although Herschel was not the first to spot Uranus, he was the first to recognize that it was not a star. Why did the astronomers who had spotted Uranus earlier than Herschel not come to this same conclusion? The reason is simple: Herschel was one of the first astronomers who became an expert at what he did. At one point in his life, he decided that he would devote all his time to mapping the heavens. Herschel is still recognized as the father of stellar astronomy. However, the first interest that he developed in life was not astronomy but music.

Pursuing a Hobby

Born in Germany on November 15, 1738, Herschel became a musician like his father and joined a military band when he was fourteen. Five years later, he moved to England, where he spent the rest of his life. His interest in music continued in his new homeland. In time, the performances and lessons he gave provided a good income. The money he earned from music allowed Herschel to devote more and more time to his hobby—astronomy.

At first, Herschel rented telescopes to study the night sky. He found them mostly useless. They were too long and produced images that were blurry and surrounded with colors. Although the quality of telescopes he rented gradually improved, none could provide him with the closer views of the stars that he wanted. There was only one solution. In 1768, he built his first telescope. He used it to map all the stars he could find.

In 1608, Hans Lippershy discovered that a distant object could be seen much more clearly if it was observed by peering at it through a series of lenses. Lippershy was a Dutch optician, someone who makes lenses. To see distant objects more clearly, Lippershy placed two lenses in a long tube and had made the first telescope. Lippershy's invention is known as a refracting telescope.

Refracting telescopes work by bending, or refracting, light by passing it through a glass lens. The image is then magnified and brought into focus. By making lenses that have just the right shape, the light coming from a distant object can be refracted, magnified, and focused so that the object appears much closer. However, refracting telescopes have one problem.

The white light coming from a planet or star is actually a composite of many colors. These colors make up the visible spectrum of light and include red, orange, yellow, green, blue, indigo, and violet. These colors can be seen in a rainbow as the white light from the Sun is refracted by tiny water drops in the air. Each color corresponds to a different wavelength. The wavelengths of red are the longest, while the wavelengths of blue are the shortest. As the various wavelengths of light pass through a lens, they are refracted differently. This is called chromatic aberration. Images in refracting telescopes of Herschel's time exhibited chromatic aberration, which surrounded planets and stars with either reddish or bluish halos.

In 1663, a Scottish astronomer named James Gregory designed a different type of telescope. Known as a reflecting telescope, Gregory's design involved bouncing, or reflecting, light off a curved mirror and then magnifying the image by passing it through a lens. Based on Gregory's design, Isaac Newton built the first reflecting telescope in 1688. Unlike lenses that refract wavelengths differently, mirrors reflect all wavelengths the same way. Therefore, reflecting telescopes do not exhibit chromatic aberration. As a result, the images seen with a reflecting telescope are not surrounded by colored halos. The telescopes Herschel used to study Uranus were reflecting telescopes.

Hans Lippershy at work in his optical shop

From that point on, Herschel's house was turned into a telescope factory. Along with his sister Caroline, whom he had brought from Germany, he spent long hours on his new passion. There were times when he would spend sixteen straight hours slowly polishing a mirror for one of his telescopes. The largest telescope he made had a 40-foot (12-meter) tube, but Herschel found it too large to aim and focus. Instead he did most of his observing through a 20-foot (6-m) telescope he had made. On the night he first spotted Uranus, Herschel was using an even smaller telescope that was only 7 feet (2 m) long.

His powerful telescope had given Herschel a clue that Uranus was not a star. It did not appear like a point of light, as a star does, but rather as a disc-shaped object. However, his devotion to astronomy and his skill at building powerful telescopes were not enough to prepare Herschel to conclude that Uranus was not a star. What was just as important was his obsession with measuring the positions of stars as accurately as possible. His mapping skills revealed that Uranus moved very slowly through the sky. His calculations showed that it moved in an orbit around the Sun that was almost circular. This is something that stars do not do.

Finding the Unexpected

Why did it take Herschel so long to recognize that Uranus was a planet? The main reason is that most people, including astronomers, believed that there were no more planets to be found. For them, the model of our solar system that Copernicus had proposed in 1543 was complete. In 1610, the Italian astronomer Galileo Galilei became the first astronomer to study the skies with a telescope. He agreed with what Copernicus had written, that there were six planets orbiting the Sun. Galileo confirmed that these planets did not travel in orbits that were perfect circles, as another astronomer, Johannes Kepler, had earlier discovered. Rather, their orbits were *ellipses,* or circles that are somewhat elongated. But all Galileo could see with his telescope were six planets. So in the 1780s, when Herschel was peering at the sky through his telescope, no one thought of looking for another planet.

Saturn

Another reason that no one had identified Uranus as a planet sooner is that astronomers at that time believed that planets were very bright objects. Even Saturn, the dimmest of the six planets known before Herschel's discovery, is still the ninth brightest object in the sky. The only brighter objects are the Sun, our Moon, the four other planets known at that time besides Earth, and the two brightest stars. Because Uranus is twice as far from Earth as Saturn, much less sunlight reaches it. As a result, Uranus appears far dimmer than Saturn. Because it is so dim and appeared more like a star, no one suspected that Uranus was a planet.

For these reasons, Herschel could not believe that he had spotted a new planet. Fortunately, other astronomers recognized what he had discovered. They convinced him that he had discovered a new planet. Although Herschel's discovery would never be known as George's Star, King George III was still grateful. Besides making Herschel his official astronomer, the king provided Herschel with an annual salary, knighted him, and gave him a lump sum of money. Herschel used the money to build his largest telescope. With his salary, he no longer had to perform and give music lessons to make a living. Now Herschel could spend all his time on astronomy.

Herschel's discovery of Uranus was only one of the many discoveries he made as an astronomer. With his sister's help, he catalogued a list of 2,500 objects beyond the solar system. This was more than ten times the number in any previous astronomy catalog. During his lifetime, he discovered about eight hundred binary, or double, stars. These are stars that orbit each other because of their mutual gravitational attraction. He also discovered that the Sun is not stationary in the sky but is moving toward a point in a constellation called Hercules. Of course, Herschel continued to study Uranus and made a number of discoveries about the planet he had found. But because it is so far from Earth, Uranus would not reveal all its secrets until scientists could get a better look at the planet. When scientists finally were able to look, they discovered something very unusual about Uranus.

False color composite of Uranus taken by *Voyager 2* on January 1, 1986.

A World on Its Side

Herschel's discovery of Uranus in 1871 nearly doubled the size of our solar system. Recall that astronomers believed that Saturn's orbit marked the outer edge of our solar system. The average distance between the Sun, the center of our solar system, and Saturn is about 900 million miles (1.4 billion km). The average distance between the Sun and Uranus is 1.8 billion miles (2.9 billion km). Uranus is slightly more than nineteen times farther from the Sun than Earth.

Before *Voyager 2* made its short visit in 1986, scientists focused their most powerful telescopes to learn whatever they could about the planet. Among their discoveries was the observation that Uranus is tilted. To understand what is meant by a planet being tilted, imagine that you push a pencil through a rubber ball. The ball represents a planet, which is spinning, or rotating, on its axis. The pencil represents a planet's axis. If the point of the pencil is pointing straight upward, then the ball represents a planet that is not tilted. Now imagine that you tilt the pencil. The ball now represents a planet that is tilted.

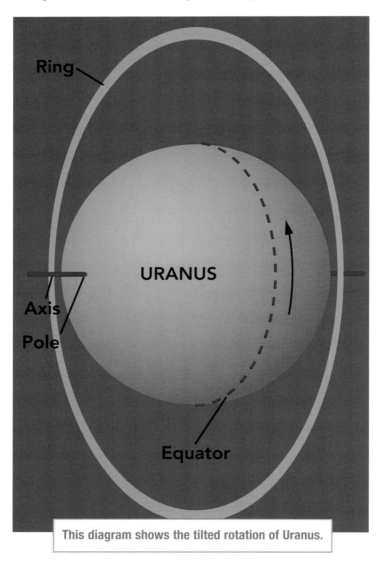

Ring

URANUS

Axis

Pole

Equator

This diagram shows the tilted rotation of Uranus.

Uranus, which is tilted 97.77 degrees, is not the only planet that is tilted. In fact, Uranus is not even the planet with the greatest degree of tilt. That honor belongs to Venus, which has a tilt of a little more than 177 degrees. A tilt of 180 degrees is half a turn. This is like turning the ball and pencil upside down.

Both Venus and Uranus are known as *retrograde rotators*. A retrograde rotator is a planet that spins on its axis in a direction opposite to the direction of its orbit. An axis of a planet runs between its north pole and south pole. If you were to look down on the north pole of Earth, you would see the planet spinning in a counterclockwise direction. However, if you were to look down on the north pole of Uranus, you would see the planet spinning in a clockwise direction. When looking north, east is to the right. Uranus, like Venus, rotates from east to west. On these two planets, the Sun rises in the west and sets in the east, the opposite of what happens on Earth. However, sunrises and sunsets on Uranus are very rare, as you will shortly learn.

Although it is not a retrograde rotator, Earth is tilted 23.45 degrees. Planets that are tilted, no matter how little or how much, have seasons. Because of its tilt, Earth has four seasons in its temperate zones—summer, fall, winter, and spring. Near the equator, the temperature does not vary much throughout the year. As a result, this zone has just a dry season and a wet season. This is very different from what happens on Uranus.

Rotating on Its Side

Uranus has a tilt of almost 98 degrees. A tilt of 90 degrees is a quarter turn. Because of its tilt, Uranus is a world on its side. At times, its north pole is almost directly in line with the Sun. At this point, its

The Geographic Poles

Like all planets, Uranus has a geographic north and a geographic south pole. The word "pole" comes from the Greek "polos," which means "hub." The hub is the part of the wheel around which everything else revolves. The geographic north and south poles are the two opposing points about which a planet rotates. Again imagine a pencil pushed through the center of a rubber ball that represents a planet. The two points where the pencil sticks out of the ball represent the geographic north and south poles.

Earth's geographic north pole is located in the Arctic, while its geographic south pole is in the Antarctic. The Earth rotates around these poles once each day.

As a result, Earth's surface and everything on it is constantly spinning. This movement is fastest at the equator, where the Earth is spinning at about 1,050 miles per hour (1,690 kph). Only the geographic poles remain still. If you were to stand on either pole, you would only turn in place.

Because Earth has a tilt of 23.45 degrees, the poles are not oriented straight up and down. If you picture a clock, the geographic north pole would be positioned between 12 and 1, while the geographic south pole would be between 6 and 7. Because Uranus has a tilt of 97.77 degrees, its geographic north pole would be positioned at a little past 3, while its geographic south pole would be a little past 9.

northern hemisphere is entirely in sunlight. Because Uranus takes about 84 Earth years to complete one orbit, its north pole will continue to point toward the Sun for some 21 Earth years. During this time, its southern hemisphere will be in complete darkness.

As it continues to orbit, Uranus reaches a point when its equator is almost directly in line with the Sun. When this happens, the whole planet is in sunlight at some point during its rotation on its axis. While Earth takes twenty-four hours (one Earth day) to complete a rotation, Uranus takes a little more than seventeen hours (one Uranian day). Sunlight will strike much of Uranus at some point during its day for about the next twenty-one Earth-years.

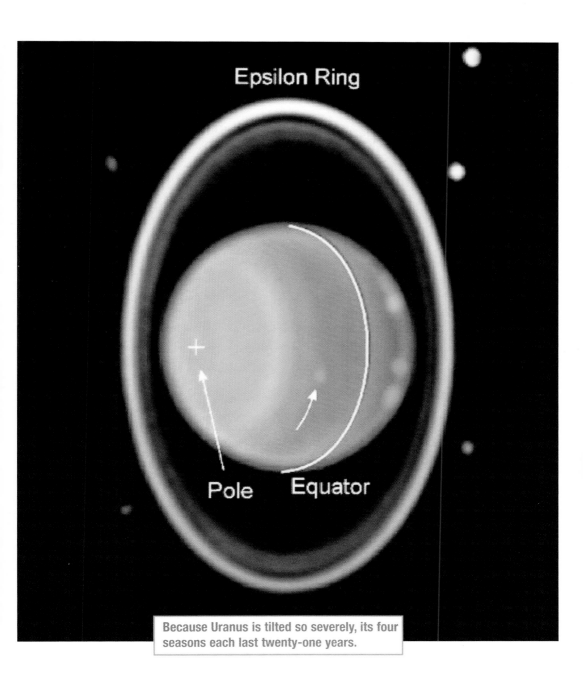

Epsilon Ring

Pole   Equator

Because Uranus is tilted so severely, its four
seasons each last twenty-one years.

Then Uranus's orbit will take it so that its south pole is pointing almost directly at the Sun. For the next twenty-one Earth-years, the southern hemisphere on Uranus will be light, while its northern hemisphere will be dark. As it completes its orbit, Uranus's equator will once again point almost directly toward the Sun. For the final twenty-one Earth-years of its orbit, much of Uranus will again be in sunlight at some point during one Uranian day. Like Earth, Uranus has four seasons. However, while each season on Earth lasts for about three months, each season on Uranus lasts for about twenty-one Earth-years.

Because Uranus is so far from the Sun, the change of seasons on the planet makes little difference in terms of temperature. Because the two poles receive more sunlight in the course of an Uranian year, they are the warmest part of the planet. Even though the poles are continuously exposed to sunlight for almost twenty-one Earth-years, they are still extremely cold. The average temperature on Uranus is −350 degrees Fahrenheit (−212 degrees Celsius).

Although the temperature does not vary much throughout an Uranian year, the change of seasons does bring about some violent changes in the weather. In 1999, a change of seasons on Uranus was photographed for the first time. The time-lapse movie was recorded by the *Hubble Space Telescope* (*HST*). The *HST* was launched into space on April 24, 1990, aboard the space shuttle *Discovery* and was released into orbit two days later. Equipped with a variety of instruments, the *HST* was designed to take a closer look into deep space. The images taken by the *HST* are much clearer than anything that can be taken from Earth.

The *HST* is in an orbit about 375 miles (600 km) above Earth. At this altitude, the *HST* is also traveling above Earth's *atmosphere*. All light coming from outer space must pass through Earth's atmosphere

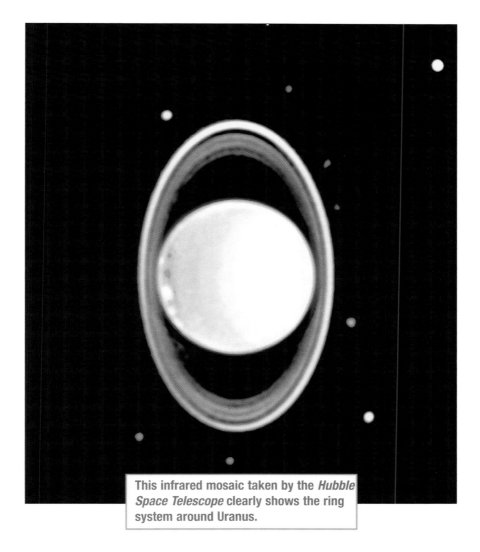

This infrared mosaic taken by the *Hubble Space Telescope* clearly shows the ring system around Uranus.

before it reaches the ground. As it does, this light bounces off the gas *molecules* that make up the atmosphere. As a result, the light is not as focused as it was when it entered the atmosphere. The more the light gets bounced around, the less it is focused. This is like the headlights of a car shining in a fog.

By the time it reaches Earth's surface where a telescope waits, this light can be so out of focus that everything becomes blurred. Above Earth's atmosphere, light does not get bounced around because there are almost no gas molecules. Because the *HST* is above Earth's atmosphere, the light it receives is much more focused than the light picked up by a telescope on the ground.

Spotting Giant Clouds

In 1999, the *HST* recorded massive clouds forming over Uranus as the part of the planet that was dark for so long moved into the dim sunlight. The temperature rose, perhaps to as high as –300° F (–184° C). This slight warming of part of the planet, along with the planet's rotation, created winds that reached 500 mph (800 kph). The clouds sped across the planet at hundreds of miles per hour. The *HST* also detected that of all the planets in the outer solar system, Uranus has the brightest clouds.

The *HST* and *Voyager 2* are the only space probes that have taken a close-up look at Uranus. Neither, however, has provided scientists with any information to explain why the planet is tilted on its side. Even so, scientists have an idea. They think that Uranus might have been knocked on its side when the planets were being formed. Over the years, several hypotheses have been suggested as to how the planets were formed. A *hypothesis* is commonly defined as an educated guess. The emphasis in this definition is on the word "educated." When a scientist proposes a hypothesis, he or she is suggesting an explanation to a question or problem. What is important to understand is that the suggested explanation comes from the information a scientist has. In other words, there is a foundation on which a hypothesis is based.

This computer-generated image of Uranus shows variations in the planet's temperature.

Forming the Solar System

Most scientists think that our solar system was formed from a gas and dust cloud known as a *nebula*. For obvious reasons, this is known as the Nebular Hypothesis. According to this hypothesis, our solar system was formed about 4.6 billion years ago. Our solar system started as a nebula, or disc-shaped cloud of dust and extremely hot gases. As the dust and gases began to be pulled inward by gravity, the nebula spun faster and faster. As it did, its *mass* began to collapse toward the center of the nebula. As the mass moved toward the center, the center of the nebula's gravity also moved inward, pulling in more dust and gases. The center of the nebula slowly filled with more and more dust and gases, eventually forming a small, glowing ball.

The temperature at the center of this ball became so great that a process called *nuclear fusion* started. Nuclear fusion occurs when atoms of one or more *elements* combine and form a different element. In this case, atoms of hydrogen gas were combined to form atoms of helium gas. In the process, huge amounts of energy were released, mostly as heat and light. This is how our Sun is thought to have formed. To this day, nuclear fusion is still occurring in our Sun.

Once the Sun was formed, some of the material from the nebula continued to swirl around it. Some of this material started to clump together. These clumps grew bigger and bigger as more and more particles were pulled in by gravity. The dust particles continued to clump. Slowly, a nebula formed a *planetesimal,* which is a very early stage in the formation of a planet. At first, a planetesimal is only a few miles or kilometers in diameter. But another planetesimal may collide with it and join to form one, larger mass. These collisions can continue until the mass gets big enough to become a planet. Forming a planet from a nebula may have taken some one hundred million years.

When planetesimals collided, they did not always join to form one, larger mass. At times, they bounced off each other after colliding. Scientists think that Uranus had been formed as a planet when it was violently knocked on its side by a very large planetesimal. Uranus has continued to orbit the Sun on its side ever since.

The crew of the space shuttle *Challenger*. Front row, from left to right: Michael Smith, Francis Scobee, Ronald McNair. Back row, from left to right: Ellison Onizuka, Christa McAuliffe, Gregory Jarvis, Judith Resnik.

First Tragedy, Then Success

On January 26, 1986, *Voyager 2* was in the last day of its Near Encounter Phase with Uranus. Scientists could hardly wait to start taking a close look at the images being sent back by the spacecraft. In fact, even the media and the public were anxious to see what the images would reveal about this distant world. But then everyone soon forgot about *Voyager 2* and Uranus. That same day in January, the space shuttle *Challenger* exploded shortly after being launched from Florida. The seven astronauts aboard were killed, making it the worst space tragedy in history. Out in deep space, *Voyager 2* continued on its journey, suddenly ignored by those on Earth.

After the initial shock of the tragedy, NASA scientists slowly returned to the job of examining the images and information sent back by *Voyager 2*. The spacecraft revealed more details about the planet than all previous Earth-based studies combined, beginning with the work of Herschel in 1781. Because Uranus is so far from Earth, early astronomers could learn little about Uranus, even with the help of their large and powerful telescopes. All a person can see when viewing Uranus through a large telescope under the best conditions is a fuzzy, blue-green disc.

Before *Voyager 2* visited Uranus, scientists knew that the planet was much smaller than Jupiter and Saturn, but still a giant compared to Earth. In 1788, Herschel calculated its diameter to be 34,025 miles (54,746 km). In the early 1970s, the diameter of Uranus was thought to be 31,393 miles (50,511 km). This is about four times the diameter of Earth, but only about one-third that of Jupiter and less than one-half that of Saturn. In 1977, scientists were able to get a more accurate measurement of Uranus's diameter. That year, Uranus passed in front of, or eclipsed, a bright star. All scientists had to do was to time how long Uranus hid the star from view. Because they knew how fast Uranus was traveling in its orbit, they could then calculate its diameter.

To get an idea of what the scientists hoped to do, imagine that you are in space looking down on a plane traveling over the United States. As the plane flies across the country, it casts a shadow on the land. Assume the plane is traveling at 500 mph (800 kph). You mark the spot on land where the plane casts its shadow. Two hours later, you mark the spot on land where the plane now casts its shadow. To find the distance on land between these two spots, all you would have to do is multiply the plane's speed by the time traveled. In this imaginary example, the distance between the two spots on land would be 500 mph (800 kph) × 2 hours, which equals 1,000 miles (1,600 km).

So all scientists had to know was how long it took for Uranus to cast its shadow over the star during the eclipse. Actually, they had to consider several other factors in their calculations, but at least they now had a way to determine Uranus's diameter more accurately. Scientists had plenty of time to prepare. Uranus's eclipse of the star had been predicted four years earlier, in 1973. Because the Southern Hemisphere would be the best spot to view the eclipse, some scientists went to observatories in Australia, while others traveled to South Africa.

Getting the Best View

Even though they were well prepared, something was still bothering the scientists. They knew that even if it were a clear night, Earth's atmosphere would still interfere with what little light came from the star that Uranus was about to eclipse. The only way to avoid this problem was to look at the eclipse from a point as far above Earth's atmosphere as possible. So several scientists asked to borrow a telescope from NASA. This telescope was quite large. In addition, it was equipped with a viewing device that had been specially designed for studying eclipses. But what was most important is that the telescope was not on Earth. It was carried by a converted military cargo jet. Known as the Kuiper Airborne Observatory, the telescope could take images of Uranus from more than 40,000 feet (12,000 m) above Earth. These images would be clearer than any taken from Earth because at that altitude there would be far less interference from the light coming from Uranus.

Based on their observations in 1977 from the observatory, scientists calculated Uranus's diameter to be 31,880 miles (51,295 km). Images from *Voyager 2* in 1986 changed this slightly. Uranus is now

The telescope aboard the Kuiper Airborne Observatory took photographs of Uranus.

thought to be 31,770 miles (51,118 km) in diameter. Recall that Herschel measured its diameter to be 34,025 miles (54,746 km). Keep in mind that Herschel was some thirty thousand times farther from Uranus than *Voyager 2*. Moreover, although he had built the best telescope of its time, it was still a primitive viewing device compared to what scientists now have available. Yet Herschel's measurement of Uranus's diameter in 1788 was only about 7 percent off from what *Voyager 2* measured nearly two hundred years later!

Measuring the Diameter

The diameter of a solid, round object, such as Earth, is the length of a straight line that passes through the center of the object. For example, Earth's diameter would be the distance from any point on its surface through its center and then straight to a point on the opposite surface. However, as you will read later, Uranus is a planet made mostly of gases and has no solid surface. As a result, scientists must use a different method to calculate the diameter of gas giants.

To calculate Uranus's diameter, scientists measure its atmospheric pressure. Atmospheric pressure is caused by gas molecules that are constantly moving in the atmosphere. You probably are familiar with a barometer that measures atmospheric pressure on Earth in either inches or millimeters of mercury. Scientists use a unit called the bar to record atmospheric pressure. The atmospheric pressure on Earth at sea level is 1 bar. The diameter of a gas planet, such as Uranus, is the distance from the center at which a pressure of 1 bar is measured.

From Uranus's diameter, scientists can calculate its *volume* or size. Volume is the amount of space the planet takes up and is measured in cubic kilometers (km³). The volume of Uranus is 6.8×10^{13} km³ (1.63×10^{13} miles³). Uranus's volume makes it the third largest planet in our solar system.

Voyager 2 sent back information not only about Uranus's volume but also about its mass. Diameter indicates how big an object is or how much space it takes up. Mass is a measurement of how much matter or "stuff" is in that space. The unit for mass is the kilogram. Scientists calculated Uranus's mass to be about 8.7×10^{25} kg. In other words, Uranus's mass is equal to 87,000,000,000,000,000,000,000,000 kilograms.

From Uranus's mass and volume, scientists could calculate its *density*. Density is the quantity of mass in a particular volume. The density of an object is calculated by dividing mass by volume. The density of Uranus is 1.27 grams/cubic centimeter (g/cm³). This number is sim-

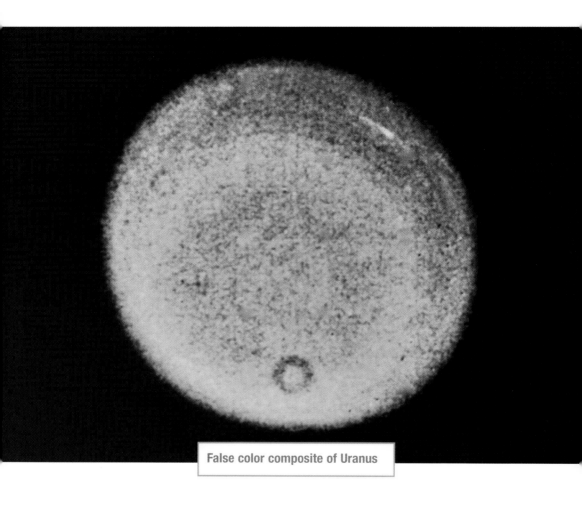

False color composite of Uranus

ilar to the densities for the other planets of the outer solar system—
Jupiter, Saturn, Neptune, and Pluto. However, the density of Uranus
is far less than those of the planets of the inner solar system—Mercury,
Venus, Earth, and Mars.

Scientists think that the difference in densities between the two
groups of planets can be explained by the processes that occurred when
the planets formed. The planets of the inner solar system are closer to

the Sun. After each planet was formed from planetesimals that combined, most of the gases in the nebula were evaporated by the Sun's heat. As a result, Mercury, Venus, Earth, and Mars are planets made mostly of rocky materials. Being much farther out in space, the planets of the outer solar system received little heat from the Sun. Their gases were not evaporated to any great extent. As a result, Jupiter, Saturn, Neptune, and Uranus are planets made mostly of gases. Pluto, by the way, is another story. Because it is so far from the Sun, Pluto retained some of its ices, giving it a higher density than the other planets of the outer solar system.

Examining Uranus's Interior

The best way to learn about the structure of Uranus is to analyze samples from the planet itself. Unfortunately, no spacecraft has ever landed on Uranus. The only clues about the planet's structure come from *Voyager 2*. Although Uranus is a gas giant, scientists think that three types of materials are present: rock, ice, and gas.

The innermost part, or core, of Uranus is thought to be made of rock. But scientists did not get enough information from *Voyager 2* to be sure that this rocky core even exists. If it does, they suspect that it makes up very little of the planet, perhaps no more than 3 percent by mass. The size of this rocky core is much smaller than that of Earth.

Surrounding this core may be a layer of ice and rock, making up about 85 percent of the planet's mass. The ice is made mostly of water, but there is probably also some methane and ammonia ice. At one time, some scientists thought that this layer was a giant ocean made of slushy ice and rock. After studying information sent back by *Voyager 2*, this was no longer the case. If Uranus did have an ocean as part of its structure, then its rapid rotation would cause the planet to bulge at its equator more than it does.

The outermost layer of Uranus is not solid. Rather, this layer is made mostly of hydrogen and helium gases. Other gases in this layer include water vapor, ammonia, and methane. All these gases are mixed together in a very dense layer that forms the surface of the planet. Like the other planets of the outer solar system, Uranus is mostly a giant ball of gases that make up its surface. As a result, a spacecraft could not land on its surface.

In studying the structure of Uranus, *Voyager 2* also confirmed an observation that Herschel had made about the planet in 1783. Like Earth's poles, Uranus's poles are also somewhat flattened. However, Uranus's poles are flatter, making its shape more elliptical and less spherical than Earth's. To get a better idea of Uranus's shape, imagine that you are holding a tiny rubber ball between two fingers. Its shape is like that of Earth. Now imagine that you are gently squeezing the ball. The top

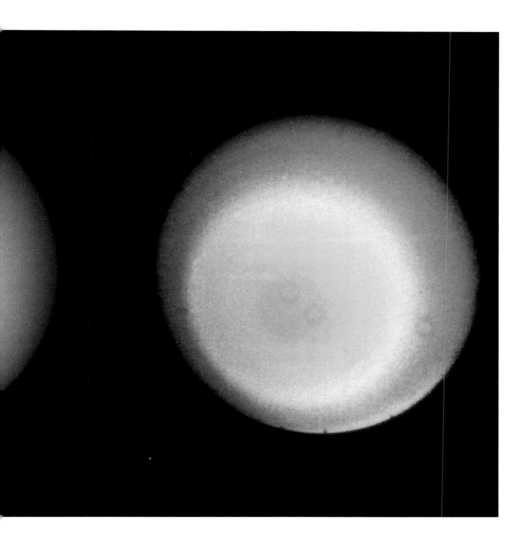

and bottom will flatten somewhat while the middle will bulge out slightly. Its shape is now like that of Uranus.

Although Herschel observed that Uranus's poles were somewhat flattened, he was not able to calculate how flattened they are. The ideal time to do so would have been in 1798, when the planet's equator was turned toward Earth and both its poles were visible. Apparently Herschel made no observations of Uranus after 1795. Prior to that year, Uranus had been tilted so that its poles were not clearly visible from Earth. As a result, trying to measure their flatness was very difficult, if not impossible.

Opportunities to again measure the poles' flatness came in 1840, 1882, and 1924. But scientists could not agree on how flat they were. Some even reported that they could not see any flatness. Finally in 1986, *Voyager 2* provided images that clearly showed that the planet's poles are flattened. Scientists concluded that Uranus, like the other planets of the outer solar system, is not as spherical in shape as the planets of the inner solar system.

When Herschel first detected that Uranus's poles were somewhat flattened, he suggested that the cause was the rapid rate at which the planet rotated. One complete rotation of a planet on its axis represents

Calculating the Oblateness

The flattening of a planet is called its oblateness. The formula for calculating a planet's oblateness is the difference between the radius to a pole and the radius to the equator divided by the radius to the equator. This can be written as the following equation.

$$oblateness = radius_{equator}$$

$$-radius_{pole}/radius_{equator}$$

Scientists have calculated Uranus's oblateness as 0.02293. This means that Uranus is flattened by 2.3 percent. In comparison, Earth's oblateness is 0.00335, meaning that the Earth is flattened by only 0.34 percent. Therefore, Uranus is flattened almost seven times more than Earth. Uranus's high oblateness confirms what scientists think about the planet's interior. If Uranus's interior were composed entirely of rocky materials like Earth, then it would not be as oblate or flattened.

the length of its day. The length of a day on Earth is twenty-four hours, the time it takes the planet to make one complete rotation. Herschel suggested that Uranus completes its rotation faster than Earth. But he was not able to say exactly how long it took because studying its rotation through a telescope from so far away is extremely difficult, even today.

The first calculation of Uranus's rotation period was made in 1856 by a French astronomer, who estimated it to be between seven and a half and twelve and a half hours. In the early 1900s, astronomers were more precise and calculated the rotation period to be about ten hours. This changed in the 1980s, when the rotation period was calculated to range anywhere from fifteen to twenty-four hours. The main problem scientists faced was the fact that they could not see a distinct feature on Uranus. If they had been able to, they could have simply timed how long it took for the feature to reappear at exactly the same spot, after the planet had completed one rotation. This would have given them the length of an Uranian day.

Finally, in 1986 *Voyager 2* provided scientists with the information they needed to calculate the rotation period of Uranus. It is 17.2 hours, or 17 hours, 14 minutes, and 24 seconds. Like the other planets of the outer solar system, Uranus rotates faster than Earth. This rapid rotation causes the equator of the planet to bulge outward and pull the two poles toward the planet's center. As a result, the distance from the center of the planet to one of its poles is shorter than the distance from the center to its equator. Besides discovering its rapid rotation, *Voyager 2* provided some other interesting surprises about Uranus.

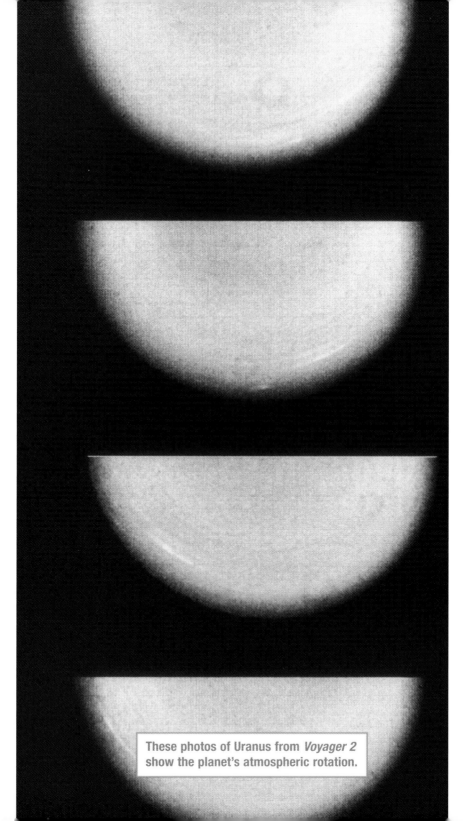

These photos of Uranus from *Voyager 2* show the planet's atmospheric rotation.

Chapter 5

Some Surprises

In December 1985, NASA scientists were becoming a little concerned about *Voyager 2*, which was some 43 million miles (69 million km) from Uranus. The spacecraft was on course and sending back images and information to Earth. But something still seemed wrong. When January came, NASA scientists began to get even more concerned. *Voyager 2* was then about 2 million miles (3.2 million km) from Uranus. But on January 24, their concern vanished. Only a little more than ten hours from its closest approach to Uranus, *Voyager 2* finally sent back what the scientists had long been waiting for—radio signals coming from the planet itself.

The scientists had expected that *Voyager 2* would pick up these radio signals soon after it left Saturn and headed for Uranus. These radio signals would indicate that Uranus has a magnetic field. You probably have used a magnet to pick up a metal object, such as a paper clip or a thumbtack. If you have, then you realize that you do not have to actually touch the metal object with the magnet to pick it up. All you have to do is bring the magnet near the object. The force of attraction extends from the magnet and draws the object to the magnet. The attractive force that extends from a magnet is called its magnetic field.

Earth acts as if it has a giant magnet buried inside. This is why the needle of a compass always points in a north-south direction. One end of the needle points toward the Earth's magnetic north pole, while the other end points toward its magnetic south pole. Scientists think that Earth is magnetic because of its core, which is deep inside its center. The core actually consists of two parts. The inner core is solid, mainly composed of iron. The outer core is a liquid mush, also made mostly of iron. This liquid, or molten, iron keeps flowing inside the core. Scientists think that this flowing, molten iron inside the core creates Earth's magnetic field that extends into space. The magnetic field of a planet that extends into space is called a *magnetosphere.*

Before *Voyager 2* headed toward Uranus, other spacecraft sent by NASA had revealed that all the planets they had studied, with the exception of Venus, have magnetospheres. The strengths of these magnetospheres vary. For example, Mercury has a weak magnetosphere, while Jupiter has a very powerful one that extends millions of miles into space. In fact, *Voyager 2* detected Jupiter's magnetosphere right after it was launched from Florida and still hundreds of millions of miles from the planet. *Voyager 2* picked up Saturn's magnetosphere soon after passing by Jupiter.

NASA scientists thus had good reason to expect that *Voyager 2* would start picking up Uranus's magnetosphere as soon as it flew past Saturn. But the spacecraft didn't detect the magnetosphere until it got very close to Uranus. Because of Uranus's mass and rotation rate, scientists expected to find a magnetosphere on Uranus. However, they are not sure why it has one. Scientists are fairly certain that Uranus, unlike Earth, does not have a core made of molten iron.

Discovering Another Tilt

Once *Voyager 2* detected Uranus's magnetosphere, NASA scientists were very surprised by the information being sent back. Uranus's magnetosphere was tilted far more than that of any other planet. Consider the situation on Earth. Recall that Earth acts as if it has a giant magnet buried deep inside itself. Like any magnet, Earth has a magnetic north pole and a magnetic south pole. The needle of a compass points to its magnetic poles. Like any planet, Earth also has a geographic north pole and a geographic south pole. Remember that these geographic poles represent the axis on which Earth rotates. The needle of a compass does not point to the geographic poles.

Earth's magnetic poles and geographic poles are not in the same location. They are separated from one another by about 11 degrees or some 300 miles (480 km). On Saturn, the magnetic and geographic poles are in the same location. On Jupiter, they are separated by about 10 degrees. But *Voyager 2* discovered that the magnetic poles on Uranus are separated from its geographic poles by almost 60 degrees, or some 4,800 miles (7,700 km).

This 60-degree separation explains why *Voyager 2* did not detect Uranus's magnetosphere until it was very close to the planet. The spacecraft was heading almost straight for the planet's geographic south pole. Because the magnetosphere was tilted so far from the axis of the geographic poles, *Voyager 2* was not on a flight path that would take it into Uranus's magnetic field until it got very close to the planet.

Scientists do not know why the two types of poles are separated by such a great distance on Uranus. Some think that the magnetic field is in the process of undergoing a reversal of its polarity. Scientists know that Earth's magnetic poles switch about every five hundred thousand to several million years. Uranus's magnetic poles may be in the process of doing the same.

In addition to a magnetosphere, *Voyager 2* also detected a *magnetotail.* A magnetotail is a magnetic field that is pushed by solar winds so that it extends behind a planet. Information collected by *Voyager 2* revealed that Uranus's magnetotail extends into space at least 6 million miles (about 10 million km) behind the planet. Because the planet has no surface features, *Voyager 2* used the magnetotail to determine the length of Uranus's rotation to be 17.2 hours. This rapid rotation twists the planet's magnetotail into a very long corkscrew shape.

Affecting the Climate

Uranus's rapid rotation has another effect. Scientists were surprised to discover that the weather on Uranus is affected by the planet's rotation and by the Sun's heating. On Earth, sunlight falls most intensely near its equator. Here, on our planet, the Sun heats the air and causes it to rise. Cooler air north and south of the equator flows in, causing winds.

Recall that because Uranus is tilted on its side, each pole receives sunlight for some twenty-one consecutive years. This should warm up the air, causing the prevailing winds on Uranus to blow north to south or south to north, depending on which pole is in the Sun. But *Voyager 2* found that the winds blow east to west because the planet rotates rapidly in that direction.

Voyager 2 also found that the temperatures around the entire planet, from poles to equator, were within a few degrees of one another. This was true no matter whether it was day or night. Apparently what little heat Uranus receives from the sunlight is spread rapidly over the planet by strong winds. The winds in the upper atmosphere of Uranus blow at 200 mph (325 kph). On Earth, winds in the jet stream blow at about half that speed. Wind speed was not the only information *Voyager 2* provided about Uranus's atmosphere.

Examining the Atmosphere

Voyager 2 also detected a few distinct clouds in the planet's atmosphere. This confirmed what some scientists had long suspected. For decades before *Voyager's* launch, a number of scientists had reported that they could see clouds on Uranus through their telescopes. However, other scientists did not observe any clouds. To spot the clouds, *Voyager 2* had to use special light filters and a computer program to enhance the contrast in the images it took. Because Uranus receives so little heat from the Sun, its few clouds lie deep in its atmosphere, making it very difficult to see them from Earth. Clouds were again spotted on Uranus by the *Hubble Space Telescope* in 1999.

Besides confirming the presence of clouds, *Voyager 2* provided scientists with information about Uranus's atmosphere. In 1934, a scientist had suggested that Uranus has a rocky core surrounded by an atmosphere. That same year, scientists obtained evidence that Uranus's atmosphere contains a gas called methane. This gas is what makes

Images taken by the *Hubble Space Telescope* revealed that the atmosphere of Uranus consisted of three layers.

Hubble's Images

In October 1998, the *Hubble Space Telescope* captured detailed images of Uranus's atmosphere. These images revealed that Uranus's atmosphere consists of three layers. The uppermost layer is made mostly of methane, while the two lower layers contain ammonia and water vapor. These layers were visible because of a special light filter used to take the images. The filter is known as an infrared filter. Infrared light, which is not visible to the human eye, has wavelengths that are longer than red light.

Interestingly, infrared light was discovered by the same person who discovered Uranus—William Herschel. In 1800, Herschel used different-colored filters to observe the Sun. He noticed that different-colored filters allowed different levels of heat to pass through them. He suspected that colors might contain different levels of heat. To test his idea, Herschel passed sunlight through a prism, which splits the light into all the colors of the rainbow. He used thermometers to measure the temperature of each color that was formed by the prism. Herschel noticed that the temperature progressively increased from the violet color to the red color. He next decided to measure the temperature just beyond the red region. To his surprise, this region had the highest temperature. Herschel discovered that this region had the properties of visible light. He called the light in the region just beyond red calorific rays. This name was later changed to infrared rays. Herschel was the first scientist to show that there is light that we cannot see with our eyes.

Uranus appear as a blue-green disc when seen from Earth. In the 1950s, a scientist suggested that Uranus's atmosphere also contains ammonia gas and water vapor. Further details about Uranus's atmosphere remained sketchy until *Voyager 2* arrived.

As scientists expected, the two main gases that make up Uranus's atmosphere are hydrogen and helium. However, *Voyager 2* detected far less helium gas than they had expected. Some studies conducted from Earth had led scientists to think that 40 percent of Uranus's atmosphere would be helium. *Voyager 2* determined it to be only 15 percent. Other gases in Uranus's atmosphere include methane, acetylene, ethane, ammonia, and water vapor.

On Earth, the temperature is cold enough for the water vapor in its atmosphere only to condense into liquid or freeze and form white clouds. All the other gases in the atmosphere, such as oxygen, nitrogen, and carbon dioxide, do not turn into liquids or solids. On Uranus, the temperature is cold enough for all the gases in its atmosphere to condense into liquids. The temperature is even cold enough for these liquids to freeze and form ice. Methane is the lightest of the gases and thus makes up the top layer of Uranus's atmosphere. When this gas condenses and freezes, the methane clouds and ice crystals that form in this top layer are the first to be struck by sunlight.

Remember that sunlight is actually a mixture of all the colors of the rainbow—red, orange, yellow, green, blue, indigo, and violet.

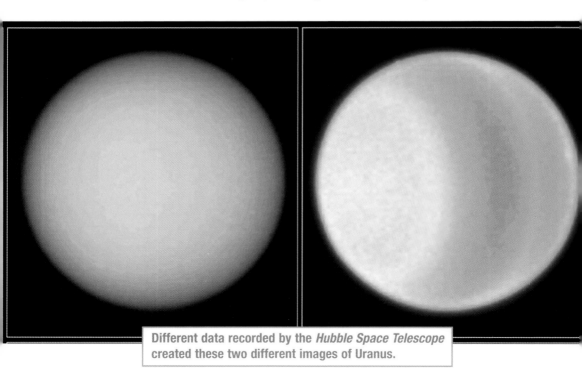

Different data recorded by the *Hubble Space Telescope* created these two different images of Uranus.

When sunlight strikes Uranus's atmosphere, the methane clouds absorb the red light and, to a lesser extent, the orange and yellow lights. The other colors of light—green, blue, indigo, and violet—are not absorbed but are reflected by the methane clouds. This is why Uranus appears blue-green.

Voyager 2 also spotted something on Uranus that is quite common in a number of places on Earth—smog. On Earth, sunlight causes certain gases in the atmosphere to react and produce a haze called *photochemical smog*. When *Voyager 2* arrived at Uranus, the planet's south pole was exposed to the Sun. The spacecraft discovered that this pole was covered with a kind of photochemical smog. Scientists think that sunlight reacts with the gases in Uranus's atmosphere, just as it does on Earth, to produce this smog. This smog also contributes to the blue-green color of Uranus.

Detecting a Glow

Another discovery that *Voyager 2* made was a glow or *aurora*. An aurora consists of natural, multicolored lights that appear in the night sky. On Earth, the two best-known auroras are the aurora borealis, which appears in very northern regions, and the aurora australis, which appears in very southern regions. Uranus has similar auroras. These auroras are caused by particles coming from the Sun that are attracted by Uranus's magnetosphere. These speeding particles are thrust into the planet's atmosphere, causing the gas molecules to glow at night.

Voyager 2 also detected another type of glow called *dayglow*. As its name suggests, dayglow is a type of aurora that appears during the day. Dayglow was first seen by *Voyager 2* on Jupiter and Saturn. So the presence of a dayglow on Uranus was not really unexpected. What did sur-

Also known as the northern lights, the aurora borealis can be seen from the northernmost regions of Earth.

prise scientists, however, was the amount of energy released by the day-glow. *Voyager 2* measured the amount of energy to be equal to a few trillion watts of power. One trillion watts is enough to supply twenty million homes with all the power they need, even during the hottest summer day. Just how Uranus generates so much power in its dayglow is still a mystery.

Voyager 2 produced still another surprise about Uranus. When the spacecraft visited Jupiter and Saturn, it revealed that these two planets give off, or radiate, almost twice the amount of energy that they receive from the Sun. This energy is released by the planets as heat, light, and radio waves that travel into space. Scientists think that most of this energy comes from the breakdown of radioactive substances present within the planets. In the case of Uranus, however, *Voyager 2* discovered that this planet radiates about 10 percent more energy than it receives from the Sun. This is even less than what Neptune radiates, as *Voyager 2* discovered when it visited this planet after it passed by Uranus. Scientists think that perhaps Uranus no longer has an internal heat source, as do Jupiter, Saturn, and Neptune. Another possibility is that Uranus has a heat source but it is covered with many layers of other materials that insulate it and prevent the heat from radiating.

An artist created this image of *Voyager 2* approaching Uranus.

Chapter 6

Another Unexpected Discovery

oyager 2 provided scientists with a number of unexpected discoveries when it flew by Uranus in 1986. The spacecraft discovered that the planet's magnetosphere was greatly tilted, just like its axis of rotation. *Voyager 2* also discovered that Uranus was rotating very quickly on its axis. Its day is nearly seven hours shorter than Earth's. The spacecraft also determined that the temperature on the planet was pretty much the same everywhere even though its poles are exposed to sunlight for nearly twenty-one consecutive Earth years. But the visit by *Voyager 2* was not the first time scientists were surprised by what they found out about Uranus. In 1977, the same year *Voyager 2* was launched, the Kuiper Airborne Observatory discovered something else quite unexpected about Uranus.

Recall that the flying observatory was being used to get a more accurate measurement of the planet's diameter during its eclipse of a bright star. The scientists were not sure of the exact time of the eclipse. So they turned on their equipment about forty-five minutes before the time they estimated it would happen. Their telescope was specifically equipped to detect the infrared light coming from the star. Most of the infrared light reaching Earth from the Sun and other stars is absorbed by Earth's atmosphere. So the best way to detect it is by getting above the atmosphere, just as the Kuiper Airborne Observatory was doing.

As expected, the infrared light from the star slowly dimmed as Uranus passed in front of it. Flying above the Indian Ocean, the scientists noticed that something else happened to the star's light. As Uranus was just about to pass in front of the star, its light flickered several times. The star's light flickered several times again just after Uranus finished its pass. Something close to the planet had temporarily blocked the light rays in their passage from the star to Earth.

At first, the scientists were puzzled as to why the star's light had flickered. But then they found out that other scientists observing Uranus from Earth also saw the star's light flicker both before and after Uranus passed in front of it. This confirmed what those on the Kuiper Airborne Observatory suspected: Uranus has a system of rings circling the planet. At that time, Saturn was the only planet known to have rings. Saturn's rings were first spotted by Galileo in 1610.

Actually, this was not the first time that Uranus had been suspected of having rings. In 1787, Herschel reported that he had spotted two opposite points near Uranus. He suggested that these two points might be parts of rings circling the planet. However, he could not eliminate the possibility that the points he saw were caused by some defect in his telescope. In 1789 and 1792, Herschel again wrote that he had observed rings around Uranus. He adjusted his telescope to see if the points disappeared. No matter what he did, he could still see what he suspected were rings around Uranus. Herschel did not think that what he saw was caused by any defects in his telescope. But in 1794 and 1795, he could not see any rings, and in 1798, Herschel finally concluded that Uranus, unlike Saturn, does not have any rings.

Herschel's difficulty in spotting the rings every time he looked is understandable. First, Uranus is much farther from Earth than Saturn, making it much more difficult to observe any features. Second, unlike Saturn's rings, which are wide and bright, those of Uranus are very narrow and dark, making them much more difficult to see. If Uranus were the size of a golf ball, its rings would be no wider than a strand in a spiderweb. Third, Uranus's rings are close to the planet, making it hard to distinguish them from the planet. Fourth, any rings would be extremely difficult to see anyway in the dim sunlight that strikes Uranus. When the camera aboard *Voyager 2* photographed Uranus's rings in 1986, it was like taking a picture at night of a small pile of charcoal at the foot of a 7-foot (2-m) tree that was lit only by a 1-watt bulb at its top.

Despite all these difficulties, it's possible that Herschel did see rings around Uranus. Then why couldn't he spot them every time he looked through his telescope? It's most likely that he saw the rings when the planet was tilted so that they were in a position to be seen from Earth. When Herschel could not spot the rings, the planet was probably tilted so that their edges were pointing toward Earth. To

Voyager 2 sent back the first photographic images of the ring system of Uranus.

understand what Herschel probably encountered, imagine that you ask someone to hold a large, flat, round object in each hand. One object is held so that you see one of its surfaces. The other object is held so that you see only its edge. Holding the objects this way, the person starts to walk away from you. At some point, the person would reach a spot where you could not see the round object held on edge but you could still see the other object.

Seeing the Light Flicker

Recall that the scientists aboard the Kuiper Airborne Observatory saw the star's light flicker several times, both before and after the eclipse. In fact, each time they saw the light flicker five times. The scientists concluded that Uranus had five rings with wide gaps between them. As each ring passed in front of the star, the star's light was blocked. Then, as the rings moved, a gap between them allowed the light to pass and produced a flicker that the scientists saw. If the light flickered five times, then there were five rings.

In 1978, scientists began photographing Uranus through their telescopes on Earth. They were interested in finding out as much as they could about the planet's rings. By 1986, they identified four more rings, bringing the total to nine. In 1986, *Voyager 2* spotted two more rings. At present, scientists know of eleven rings that circle Uranus. Working outward from the planet, they are named 1986U2R, 6, 5, 4, Alpha, Beta, Eta, Gamma, Delta, 1986U1R, and Epsilon.

Unlike those of Saturn, the rings around Uranus are all extremely narrow. They are between 26,000 and 32,000 miles (41,834 and 51,488 km) from the center of Uranus. The eight innermost rings are nearly circular and less than 7 miles (11 km) wide. Epsilon, the outermost ring, has a more elliptical shape and its width varies between 12 and 59 miles (19 and 95 km). All the rings circle the equator of Uranus. When one of its poles is pointed toward Earth, Uranus and its rings look like a gigantic bull's-eye with the planet in the center. This

Naming the Rings

Although they may not look like it, the names of ten of Uranus's rings are official. These names have been officially approved by the International Astronomical Union (IAU) Nomenclature Commission. Only 1986U2R has not been given an official name. The IAU's decision is based in part on the observation that 1986U2R, unlike the other ten rings, is made of very tiny dust particles. The particles that make up the others rings are large enough so that these rings can be seen through Earth-based telescopes.

However, 1986U2R is unique in that it is the widest of all eleven rings, with a width of approximately 1,550 miles (2,500 km). The next widest is Epsilon, whose width is between 12 and 59 miles (19 and 95 km). With the exception of Epsilon, the thickness of each ring is about 0.06 miles (100 m). The thickness of Epsilon is somewhat less than 0.09 miles (150 m). The following table lists some information about the eleven known Uranian rings.

Name	Distance (as measured from the center of Uranus to start of ring)	Width
1986U2R	38,000 km	2,500 km
6	41,837 km	1–3 km
5	42,235 km	2–3 km
4	42,571 km	2–3 km
Alpha	44,718 km	4–13 km
Beta	45,661 km	7–12 km
Eta	47,176 km	1–2 km
Gamma	47,627 km	1–4 km
Delta	48,300 km	3–7 km
Lambda	50,024 km	2–3 km
Epsilon	51,149 km	19–95 km

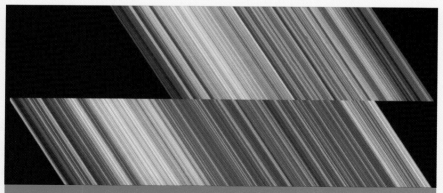

Two slices of Uranus's epsilon ring are shown in this image created from data from the photographs taken by *Voyager 2*.

is how Uranus and its rings were positioned when *Voyager 2* arrived. The spacecraft flew past the outermost ring, sending back the first detailed information about the rings' structure.

All the rings are as black as coal. They appear to be made of particles of rock and ice with diameters greater than 3 feet (1 m). The rock particles may be coated with black carbon. The ice particles made be made of frozen methane, which turns black when exposed to sunlight. Most of the little sunlight that does strike these darkened particles is absorbed. Because very little of the sunlight is reflected, the rings are quite dark and difficult to spot, especially from a vast distance. Even Epsilon, the brightest of the rings, reflects less than 2 percent of the sunlight that strikes it. In contrast, the two brightest of Saturn's rings reflect nearly 60 percent of the sunlight that strikes them.

Falling Down

Voyager 2 did not detect any tiny dust particles in the rings circling Uranus. This is very different from Saturn and Jupiter, whose rings, with one exception, contain large amounts of dust particles. Scientists suspect that the lack of dust particles may be a sign that Uranus's rings are slowly disappearing. The much larger particles of rocks and ice that make up each ring constantly collide with one another as they circle the planet. When they do, these particles break up into smaller fragments, some as tiny as dust particles. In the case of Jupiter and Saturn, these dust particles continue to orbit the planet as part of its rings. However, on Uranus, these dust particles appear to be falling to the planet, attracted by its gravity. *Voyager 2* discovered that Uranus's atmosphere extends all the way out through its rings. This dense atmosphere slows the tiny dust particles traveling in the rings. Once they are slowed enough, Uranus's gravity can pull the dust particles toward the planet, removing them from the rings.

In time, the rock and ice particles that make up Uranus's rings may all turn into dust. All this dust will be slowed by Uranus's dense atmosphere and gradually fall toward the planet. If and when the rings are gone, however, there will still be a number of other objects orbiting Uranus. In fact, it is these objects that are thought to be responsible for keeping the rings in place as they circle Uranus. It's like a shepherd who keeps the members of a flock in place while they move. These objects act just like shepherds, keeping the rock and ice particles in place as they orbit Uranus in eleven separate rings.

Chapter 7

The Shepherds

Scientists are not sure how Uranus's rings formed. They are not even sure when they formed. The rings may have formed at the same time as Uranus, several billion years ago. But the fact that the rings are so narrow led scientists at first to believe that they formed much later than the planet. The scientists reasoned that if the rings had formed at the same time as Uranus, then the particles making up the rings should have spread out more than they have. In other words, the rings should be much wider than they are.

But scientists began to suspect that the rings did form at the same time as Uranus. Perhaps there was some external force acting like a shepherd to keep the particles in place and cause the rings to remain

The specks on this *Voyager 2* image of the rings of Uranus are backlit dust particles.

narrow. In 1979, two scientists proposed that Uranus's system of narrow rings was maintained by "shepherding satellites." A *satellite* is a natural or human-made object that orbits another body, such as a planet. The Moon, for example, is a satellite of Earth. These satellites that act like shepherds are actually some of the moons of Uranus.

Not surprisingly, Herschel was the first to discover that Uranus has moons. In 1787, he spotted two moons with his 20-foot (6-m) -long telescope. One evening, he followed the course of one of the moons as it orbited Uranus. Finally, at 3 A.M., Herschel quit, not because he was tired but because he could no longer see the moon, as Uranus had moved out of his line of sight. Herschel had no sense of urgency in naming the moons he had discovered. The names were finally provided by his son John around 1852, almost seventy years after they were first spotted. Breaking with tradition, Uranus's moons are not named after figures in Greek and Roman mythology. Herschel's son suggested that the moons be named Oberon and Titania, after two figures in William Shakespeare's play *A Midsummer Night's Dream*.

Although Herschel was in no hurry to name the moons, he was most anxious to learn as much as he could about them. For a year following his discovery, Herschel measured the speed at which they orbited Uranus. He calculated that Oberon, the outer moon, took 13.462 days to complete one orbit. Titania, being closer to Uranus, took 8.709 days. Herschel's observations and calculations, which were completed in 1788, are quite impressive. Modern-day scientists have calculated the period of Oberon's orbit to be 13.463 days and that of Titania to be 8.704 days. In Oberon's case, Herschel was off by 0.001 day or about 86 seconds for a period that lasted almost two weeks!

How Many Moons?

In December 2001, the IAU concluded that there was not enough information to declare that the object known as 1986U10 was definitely a moon of Uranus. This object was observed in seven images taken by *Voyager 2* in 1986. Surprisingly, the object was not noticed at that time. Some thirteen years later, in 1999, a scientist was examining several *Voyager 2* images to compare them to ones taken that year by the Hubble Space Telescope. It was then that the object was spotted in the *Voyager 2* images and designated a moon of Uranus with the name 1986U10. This moon appeared to be in nearly the same orbit as Belinda, a moon about 47,000 miles (75,000 km) from Uranus. Scientists calculated the diameter of 1986U10 to be about 25 miles (40 km).

However, 1986U10 has not been seen since *Voyager 2* passed by Uranus in 1986. Even the images taken in 1999 by the Hubble Space Telescope do not show the ring 1986U2. As a result, the IAU concluded that it was premature to state that Uranus has twenty-one moons. The status of 1986U10 will be reevaluated when the Hubble Space Telescope takes more images of Uranus's moons. However, that may not happen for several years, depending on how scientists schedule what the HST will examine in space. In the meantime, here is a complete list of the remaining twenty moons of Uranus, beginning with the one closest to the planet: Cordelia, Ophelia, Bianca, Cressida, Desdemona, Juliet, Portia, Rosalind, Belinda, Puck, Miranda, Ariel, Umbriel, Titania, Oberon, Caliban, Sycorax, Prospero, Setebos, and Stephano.

For about the next twenty years, Herschel continued to look for more moons that were orbiting Uranus. He reported spotting four more. Three of these were never spotted by any other astronomer. The remaining one was never accepted as being a moon by his fellow astronomers. Even Herschel's son joined in the search for more moons, but without any success.

Then in 1851, an English astronomer named William Lassell discovered two more moons. These were named Ariel, from Shakespeare's *The Tempest,* and Umbriel, from Alexander Pope's *The Rape of the Lock.* Shortly after these moons were discovered, John Herschel suggested that Umbriel had actually been first spotted by his father in 1798. Lassell disagreed, pointing out that Umbriel was much dimmer and closer to Uranus than Oberon and Titania. Lassell argued that Herschel could never have spotted Umbriel with his 20-foot (6-m) -long telescope. In 1981, a scientist closely reexamined Herschel's records and reported that on the night of April 17, 1801, Herschel did in fact spot Umbriel, fifty years before Lassell.

Scientists now concede that William Herschel may have spotted Umbriel, one of the moons of Uranus, seen here in a *Voyager 2* image.

No matter who was first to spot it, Umbriel, along with Oberon, Titania, and Ariel, remained the only moons known to be orbiting Uranus until 1948. That year, an American scientist named Gerard Kuiper spotted a fifth moon and named it Miranda, after another character in *The Tempest*. In 1986, *Voyager 2* spotted ten more moons, bringing the total to fifteen. In 1997, two more were discovered by scientists with their Earth-based telescopes. In 1999, four more moons were identified. As of today, Uranus has twenty-one known moons, more than any other planet.

Looking at the Moons

All of Uranus's moons form two distinct groups based on their size. One group consists of the first five moons that were discovered. These are the largest and thus the easiest ones to spot from Earth. The largest moon is Titania, whose diameter measures 1,000 miles (1,600 km). The other sixteen moons are all rather small. The smallest is Cordelia, with a diameter of only 16 miles (26 km). But even Titania is relatively small. For example, our Moon is 2,160 miles (3,475 km) in diameter. If our Moon were hollow, it would be possible to put all twenty-one Uranian moons inside it. Of the four giant planets in the outer solar system, Uranus is the only one without a relatively large moon.

All of Uranus's moons travel around Uranus in nearly circular orbits. Cordelia is the closest, traveling in an orbit about 30,950 miles (49,800 km) from the center of Uranus. The farthest is Stephano, whose orbit is about 15.6 million miles (25.1 million km) from the planet's center. The moons appear to rotate on their axes in the same amount of time as it takes them to revolve. As a result, each moon keeps the same side facing Uranus, just as our Moon keeps the same side facing Earth.

Like the eleven rings, all of the moons revolve around Uranus's equator, contributing to the giant bull's-eye pattern when one of the planet's poles is facing Earth. Recall that when *Voyager 2* arrived at Uranus, this is how the planet appeared. The spacecraft's target was a point just inside Miranda's orbit. This point was picked as the target not because scientists felt that Miranda might be the most interesting moon to examine, but so that *Voyager 2* could get as close to Uranus as possible and thus get a boost from the planet to send it on to Neptune, the last planet it would visit. Because of the path in space that *Voyager 2* followed, the spacecraft did not fly close to any of the other moons. As a result, the images *Voyager 2* took of the five largest moons were clearer than those of the smaller ones.

Finding the Unexpected

Scientists had expected to find the small moons dark and dull. The brightness of an object in space is called its *albedo*. The albedo is a measurement of how much of the sunlight that strikes that object is reflected by its surface. For example, the albedo of our Moon is about 12 percent. This means that the Moon reflects about 12 percent of the sunlight that strikes it. Scientists calculated that all the small moons have albedos close to those of the particles making up the rings. They have extremely dark surfaces. Puck, the brightest of the small moons, has an albedo of 7 percent. Apparently, these small moons have no obvious visible surface features and are made of rock and water ice that absorb almost all the sunlight that strikes them.

Keep in mind, however, that all these moons were showing only one of their sides to *Voyager 2* as it flew past. It is possible that their other sides may be quite different. Consider Earth, where one side of the world consists mostly of the vast Pacific Ocean while the opposite side is dominated by continents. To see if opposite sides on Uranus's small moons are different, scientists must wait until about 2025, when the moons will have their other poles pointed toward Earth.

Observing the five larger moons from Earth, scientists noticed that they were much brighter than the particles in the rings. So it was no surprise when *Voyager 2* revealed that these moons had much higher albedos than those of the smaller moons. Umbriel, the darkest of the larger moons, has an albedo of 21 percent. Ariel, the brightest, has an albedo of 39 percent. The relative brightness of the larger moons is not due to their size. Rather, it indicates that their surfaces are covered with light-colored materials. Just what these materials are remains unknown.

Miranda, the closest large moon to Uranus, turned out to have the most surprises. Miranda's surface is covered with features. In fact, nowhere in our solar system have scientists observed so many different landforms in such a small area. The smallest of the five largest moons, Miranda has a diameter of 300 miles (475 km). Large and small *craters* dot its surface. This is all scientists had expected to see. But *Voyager 2* revealed three huge, egg-shaped regions that together cover half or more of its surface. These regions have only a few craters that are criss-crossed by ridges, valleys, and deep canyons. Many of the canyons are arranged in rows. In one area, they form an oval racetrack pattern as seen from space. In another area, they look like a giant check mark. The canyons are 6 to 12 miles (10 to 20 km) deep, which is ten times deeper than the Grand Canyon. A rock dropped from the top of a canyon would take ten minutes to reach the bottom.

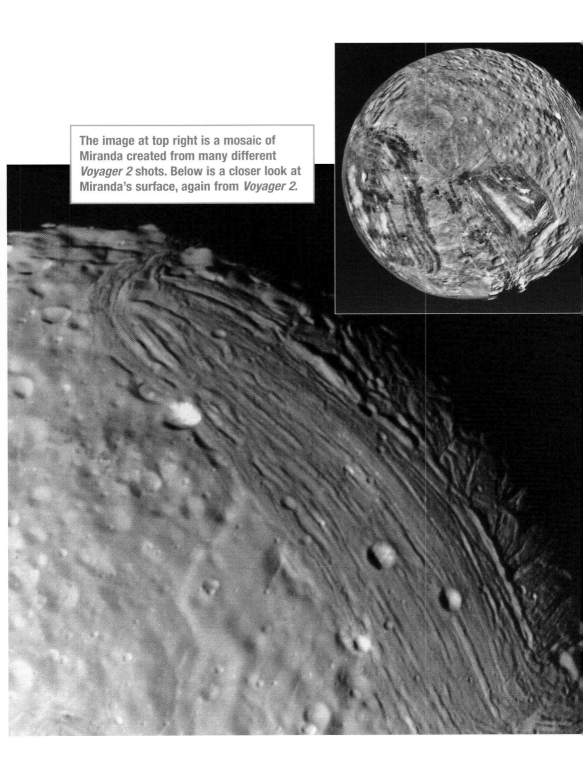

The image at top right is a mosaic of Miranda created from many different *Voyager 2* shots. Below is a closer look at Miranda's surface, again from *Voyager 2*.

Ariel, the next large moon in orbit from Uranus, is covered with valleys that extend most of the way around the moon. These valleys crisscross and are up to 20 miles (32 km) deep in some places. The floors of these valleys appear to be smooth, as if covered by some frozen fluid. Ariel is also pitted with craters, most about 6 miles (10 km) or less across. Very few large craters, like those on Miranda, are present on Ariel. Most of its surface has been smoothed over by ice and volcanic rock.

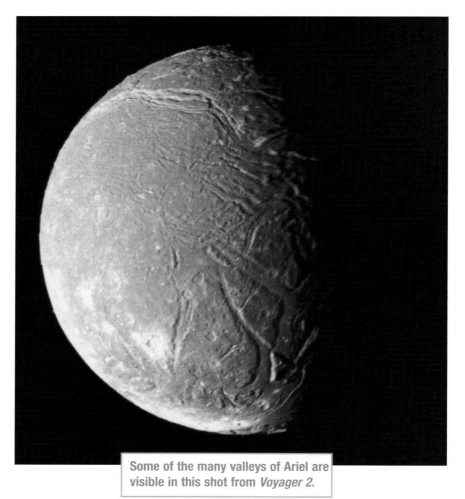

Some of the many valleys of Ariel are visible in this shot from *Voyager 2*.

Umbriel, the next moon out from Uranus, is the darkest of the large moons. Umbriel is covered with craters, many of them 50 to 100 miles (80 to 160 km) across. Little else can be seen except for two bright features. One is a ring, about 50 miles (80 km) in diameter, that covers the floor of one crater. The other is a sloping wall of another crater.

Titania, the next in order from Uranus, appears similar to Ariel. Titania's surface is a mixture of craters and valleys that are hundreds of miles long. This moon is also streaked with *faults* and cracks. Some of

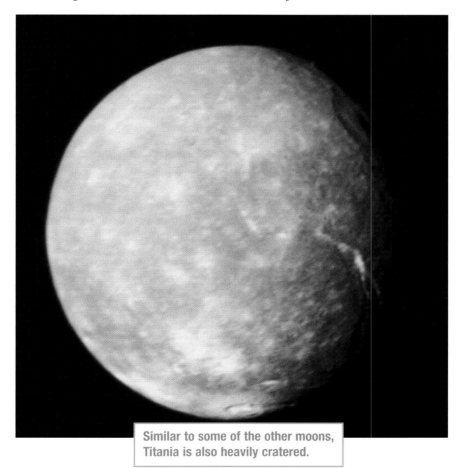

Similar to some of the other moons, Titania is also heavily cratered.

the faults stretch some 1,000 miles (1,600 km) over the moon's surface and are 45 miles (72 km) wide in some places. This is about five times wider than the Grand Canyon.

Oberon, the large moon farthest from Uranus, is heavily cratered. Many of the craters have dark floors. Perhaps some lava seeped to the surface where it hardened to cover the craters' floors. One crater contains a mountain some 12 miles (20 km) high. This is twice the height

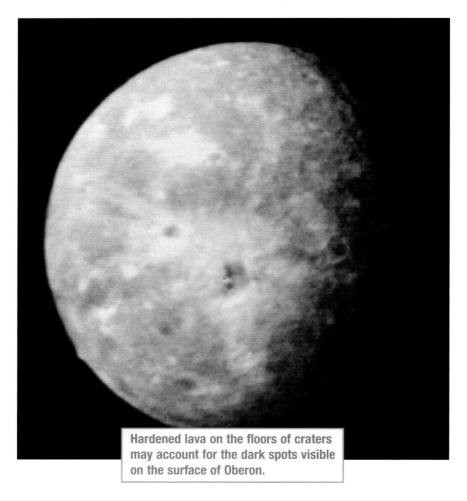

Hardened lava on the floors of craters may account for the dark spots visible on the surface of Oberon.

of Mount Everest on a moon that is only one-eighth the diameter of Earth. Because the surface is basically covered only with craters, scientists know that very little has happened on Oberon since it formed. In contrast, the other four large moons have undergone much geologic activity, to the surprise of scientists.

Shepherding the Rings

Scientists think that Uranus's moons act to keep its rings narrow by preventing the particles of rock and ice from spreading out. The particles in each ring are kept in position by probably two moons that act as shepherds. The rock and ice particles inside each ring are constantly colliding with one another. As a result, some particles slow down and thus should fall into lower orbits. Collisions may cause other particles to gain speed and thus rise to higher orbits. In time, each ring should spread out as particles move to both lower and higher orbits. Here is where the two moons affect what happens to the rings.

One moon orbits just inside the ring. The closer an object is to the body it orbits, the faster it travels. Because this moon is closer to Uranus, it travels faster than the ring outside it. Every time the moon passes a particle inside the ring, the moon gives the particle a little push. So rather than slowing down after a collision and falling to a lower orbit, the particle gains a little extra speed and stays inside the ring.

A second moon orbits just outside the ring. Because it is farther from Uranus, this moon travels more slowly than the particles inside the ring below. Every time a particle is sent speeding out of the ring for a higher orbit, this moon slows it down. As a result, the particle falls back into the ring, where it keeps on orbiting Uranus.

If there are eleven rings, and each ring needs two shepherd moons, then there should be at least twenty-two moons orbiting Uranus. Earth-based scientists have discovered eleven moons. *Voyager 2* discovered ten, bringing the total to twenty-one moons. There very well may be other moons lurking in orbit around Uranus. They are likely too small and too dark to be spotted from Earth. The only way to find them would be to send another spacecraft to Uranus. Unfortunately, there are no plans to do so. *Voyager 2* is likely to be the only spacecraft to visit Uranus in our lifetime.

Heading for Deep Space

After it flew by Uranus, *Voyager 2* next headed for Neptune, where it arrived during the summer of 1989. Interestingly, 150 years earlier, scientists had predicted that another planet existed beyond Uranus even before spotting it. This prediction was based on Uranus's orbit. After studying its orbit, scientists discovered that Uranus wandered somewhat as it circled the Sun. In 1834, scientists proposed that another planet must be out there, pulling on Uranus with its gravity. In 1846, Neptune was discovered.

In 1986, *Voyager 2* visited Uranus. In 1989, *Voyager 2* flew by Neptune. Today, *Voyager 2* is heading for the outer boundary of our solar system. Traveling at 35,000 miles per hour (56,000 kph), *Voyager 2* will eventually reach the Oort cloud, where small comets are barely held in orbit by the Sun's gravity. It will take nearly twenty thousand years for *Voyager 2* to reach the Oort cloud. By then, *Voyager 2* will have traveled a little less than half the distance to Proxima Centauri, which is a star 4.2 light-years from our Sun.

Voyager 2 took this shot of Uranus as it was leaving the planet's orbit.

Comparing Uranus to Earth

Vital Statistics

	Uranus	Earth	Uranus/Earth Ratio
MASS	8.7×10^{25} kg	5.97×10^{24} kg	14.5
VOLUME	6.8×10^{13} km³	1.08×10^{12} km³	63.1
DENSITY	1.27 g/cm³	5.515 g/cm³	0.23
EQUATORIAL RADIUS	25,559 km	6,378.1 km	4.00
POLAR RADIUS	24,973 km	6,356.8 km	3.93
OBLATENESS	0.02293	0.00335	6.84
AVERAGE ORBITAL VELOCITY	6.81 km/s	29.78 km/s	0.229
ORBITAL PERIOD	90.570 days	365.2 days	248
LENGTH OF DAY	17.24 hours	24 hours	0.718
AXIAL TILT	97.77 degrees	23.45 degrees	4.169
PERIHELION	2.74 x 109 km	1.47 x 108 km	18.6
APHELION	3.00 x 108 km	1.52 x 108 km	19.7
AVERAGE DISTANCE FROM THE SUN	2.9 x 109 km	1.5 x 108 km	19.3
NUMBER OF SATELLITES	21	1	

Vital Statistics

	Uranus	Earth	Uranus/ Earth Ratio
RING SYSTEM	yes	no	
MAGNETOSPHERE	yes	yes	
AVERAGE TEMPERATURE	−320° F (−196° C)	59° F (15° C)	

Exploring Uranus: A Timeline

1690 — Uranus is first spotted by John Flamsteed, who thinks it is a star.

1713–71 — Uranus is spotted a number of times by other astronomers, who all believe it to be a star.

1781 — William Herschel observes Uranus, first thinking that it is a comet and then agreeing with other astronomers that it is a planet.

1787 — Herschel discovers Uranian moons Titania and Oberon. He also reports observing what he suspects are rings.

1788 — Herschel makes the first measurement of Uranus's diameter.

1851 — William Lassell discovers Uranian moons Ariel and Umbriel.

1856 — A French astronomer proposes that one rotation of Uranus takes between seven and a quarter and twelve and a half hours.

1902	— A French astronomer reports that Uranus is a retrograde rotator.
1934	— The first model of Uranus's structure, including a rocky core, is proposed. Uranus's atmosphere is found to contain methane gas.
1948	— Gerard Kuiper discovers Uranian moon Miranda.
1977	— James Elliot, aboard the Kuiper Airborne Observatory, discovers the rings of Uranus that may have first been spotted by Herschel.
1977	— *Voyager 2* is launched from Cape Canaveral, Florida, and begins its long journey to Uranus.
1986	— *Voyager 2* makes its closest approach to Uranus, discovering ten small moons, two rings, a magnetosphere, clouds, and a rotation period of 17.2 hours.
1997	— Two more moons orbiting Uranus are discovered.
1999	— The Hubble Space Telescope provides images of clouds and a spring storm on Uranus. Four more moons are identified.

albedo—the measurement of the percent of sunlight reflected by an object in outer space

astronomer—a scientist who studies space

atmosphere—the layer of gases that surrounds a planet

aurora—a diffuse glow of multicolored lights that appear in the night sky; produced by particles striking gas atoms in Earth's atmosphere

comet—a ball of rock and ice that travels around the Sun from the outer edges of the solar system

crater—a bowl-shaped depression formed by the impact of a falling body

dayglow—the glow formed by large amounts of ultraviolet light

density—the ratio of mass to volume or the quantity of mass in a given volume; usually expressed in grams per cubic centimeter (g/cm^3)

element—a building block of matter

ellipse—an elongated, or somewhat flattened, circle

fault—a crack in a planet's crust along which movement has occurred

gravity—the force of attraction between two objects that depends on the masses of and the distance between the two objects

hypothesis—an educated guess that a scientist develops to explain observations and form the basis for future work

infrared light—a type of light not visible to our eyes that has wavelengths longer than visible light

magnetosphere—a region of the magnetic field of a planet that extends far out into space

magnetotail—a magnetic field that is pushed by solar winds so that it extends behind a planet

mass—the quantity of matter that makes up an object

molecule—a particle that makes up many substances, including water and the gases in the atmosphere

nuclear fusion—the combination of two elements to form a different element with more mass

orbit—the path an object follows while traveling around another object in space

photochemical smog—the haze produced when sunlight causes certain molecules in the atmosphere to react

planetesimals—small, rocky objects that may come together to form a planet

radioactive element—an element that spontaneously breaks apart and releases radiation

retrograde rotator—a planet that spins on its axis in the opposite direction of the majority of planets and in an opposite direction to its orbit

satellite—a natural or human-made object that orbits another object in space. Planets are satellites of stars, and moons are satellites of planets.

solar system—the Sun and all the objects that orbit it, including the planets

volume—the space an object takes up

To Find Out More

Books

Bergstralh, Jay T., And Ellis D. Miner. *Uranus*. Tucson, Ariz.: University of Arizona Press, 1991.

Burgess, Eric. *Uranus and Neptune: The Distant Giants*. New York: Columbia University Press, 1988.

Hunt, Garry E. *Atlas of Uranus*. Cambridge, Mass.: Cambridge University Press, 1989.

Kolb, Rocky. *Blind Watchers of the Sky*. Cambridge, Mass.: Perseus Publishing, 1996.

Littmann, Mark. *Planets Beyond: Discovering the Outer Solar System*. New York: John Wiley & Sons, 1988.

Miner, Ellis D. *Uranus: The Planet, Rings, and Satellites*. West Sussex, England: Ellis Horwood Limited, 1990.

Shepherd, Donna Walsh. *Uranus*. Danbury, Conn.: Franklin Watts, 1994.

Thompson, Luke. *Uranus*. New York: Powerkids Press, 2001.

Organizations and Online Sites

Jet Propulsion Laboratory

http://jpl.nasa.gov

Click on "Solar System" and then "Welcome to the Planets." At this site, you can see the best images from NASA's planetary exploration program, including those taken of Uranus by *Voyager 2*.

NASA Press Release: Uranus

http://science.msfc.nasa.gov/newhome/headlines/ast29mar99_1.htm

Read about the huge storms that took place on Uranus and were photographed by the *Hubble Space Telescope*. You will be able to view what "no one has ever seen . . . in the modern era of astronomy" until now.

NASA Uranus

http://pds.jpl.nasa.gov/planets/welcome/uranus.htm

Check out NASA's latest facts about Uranus.

NSSDC Photo Gallery

http://nssdc.gsfc.nasa.gov/photo_gallery

This site contains numerous photographs of the major objects in space, including Uranus, as well as photos taken by *Voyager 2*.

The Planetary Society

http://planetary.org
65 North Catalina Avenue
Pasadena, CA 91106-2301
Among the many links is one that provides a list of space-related
events from around the world.

Princeton Planetary Society

http://www.princeton.edu/~space
This site has a student organization for anyone interested in astronomy or space-related topics. You can be added to the mailing list by
writing to space@princeton.edu.

Sky and Telescope Magazine

http://skyandtelescope.com
This site offers a weekly news section on space-related topics. You
can also find tips for amateur astronomers. A list of science muse-
ums, planetariums, and astronomy clubs organized by state can help
you find nearby places to visit.

Uranus

http://solarviews.com/eng/uranus.htm
This comprehensive site has statistical information about Uranus, its
eleven rings, and its twenty-one moons.

Voyager Gee-Whiz
http://vraptor.jpl.nasa.gov/voyager/vgrfaqs.html
Learn more about the *Voyager* project, including information about its navigation systems and their most important parts.

Places to Visit

American Museum of Natural History
Rose Center for Earth and Space
Central Park West at 79th Street
New York, NY 10024-5192
http://amnh.org/rose
Check out the floor plans and show times and take a peek at the displays to get an idea of what you can see during your visit.

Exploratorium
3601 Lyon Street
San Francisco, CA 94123
http://exploratorium.edu
This science center features interactive exhibits, including space-related subjects.

Jet Propulsion Laboratory
4800 Oak Grove Drive
Pasadena, CA 91109
http://jpl.nasa.gov

This laboratory is the primary center for all NASA planetary missions. To arrange a visit, click on "Education" and then "About JPL Education."

National Air and Space Museum
7th and Independence Avenues, SW
Washington, DC 20560
http://www.nasm.edu/nasm/planetarium
Visit the Albert Einstein Planetarium, where you can tour our universe through images projected on its 70-foot (21-m) -diameter dome.

Index

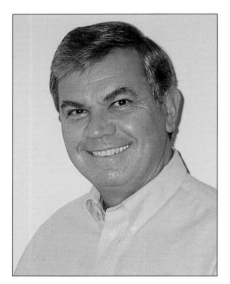

Salvatore Tocci taught high school and college science for almost 30 years. He has a B.A. degree from Cornell University and a Master of Philosophy degree from The City University of New York.

He has written books that deal with a range of science topics, from biographies about famous scientists to a high school chemistry text. He has also traveled throughout the United States to present workshops at national science conventions to show teachers how to emphasize the applications of scientific knowledge in our everyday lives.

Mr. Tocci lives in East Hampton, New York, with his wife, Patti. Both retired from teaching, they spend their leisure time sailing and traveling. On a recent trip to Florida, they went to Cape Canaveral to see a shuttle launch. Unfortunately, it was postponed.